the celtic way
of life

First published 1976 by O'Brien Educational, 20 Victoria Road, Dublin 6.
Reprinted 1977, 1978, 1982, 1984, 1985, 1987, 1988

ISBN 0-905140-16-8

The Curriculum Development Unit was established in 1972. It is funded by the City of Dublin Vocational Education Committee. It is managed jointly by the City of Dublin Vocational Education Committee, Trinity College, Dublin and the Department of Education. This book forms part of the Humanities Curriculum.

The Humanities Team: Tony Crooks (1972 —) Co-ordinator, Nora Godwin (1973 —), Agnes McMahon (1975 —), Unit Director Anton Trant.

The Celtic Way of Life has been edited for publication by Agnes McMahon.

Prior to the publication, the following schools were involved in the development, use and revision of the collection. The suggestions and comments of the teachers in these schools have been used as a basis for the edition: Colaiste Eanna, Cabra; Colaiste Eoin, Finglas; Coolmine Community School, Clonsilla; Scoil Ide, Finglas; Vocational School, Ballyfermot; Vocational School for Boys, Clogher Road; Vocational School, Crumlin Road.

Illustrations Jeanette Dunne, Cover Design, Jarlath Hayes,

Previous page: Pendant, made of tinned bronze was probably suspended at the end of a leather strap. Found on Feltrim Hill near Malahide, Co. Dublin, it dates to 4th century A.D.

the celtic way of life

CURRICULUM DEVELOPMENT UNIT

O'BRIEN

ACKNOWLEDGEMENTS

We would like to thank Áine Hyland, Anne Gill and Brian Kavanagh for work in the development of the materials: Tim O'Neill for reading and commenting on the manuscript, the Editor of the Proceedings of the Royal Irish academy for permission to quote from J. J. Tierney, "The Celtic Ethnology of Posidonius" (P.R.I.A., 1960), Mrs. Sheehy for kind permission to include The Hermit's Song, The King of Connaught, Jealousy, and Oisín, from *Kings Lords & Commons* by Frank O'Connor published by Macmillan of London; Dr. Brendan Kennelly for kind permission to include The Old Woman of Beare, A Love Song and My Story. We would like to thank Dr. Joseph Raftery, Director of the National Museum of Ireland for his generous assistance.

ILLUSTRATIONS

We are grateful to the following for permission to reproduce the illustrations in Celtic Society (The Celtic Way of Life and The Ulster Cycle). All the photographs are courtesy of the National Museum of Ireland except on page 61, courtesy Commissioners of Public Works, Ireland and page 17 courtesy Dr. J. K. St. Joseph, University of Cambridge. The photographs on pages 19 and 21 are by kind permission of the Craggaunowen Project, Shannon Free Airport Development Company Ltd. We thank Alf Mac Lochlainn, Director of the National Library of Ireland for permission to reproduce the map on page 8.

In a few instances we have not succeeded in making contact with copyright holders and would be grateful if they would write to the publishers.

contents

who were the celts?

HE CELTS came from Central Europe, an area east of the river Rhine and north of the Alps, the lands now called Bavaria and Bohemia. They were a farming people, brave and warlike, and from time to time groups of them would set out to find new lands to settle and people to conquer. They spread out in all directions, into France and Spain in the west, into Ireland and Britain in the north, into Italy in the south, into Greece and Turkey in the east; and from about 450 B.C. to 250 B.C. they were the most powerful people in Europe.

Historians are not certain when the Celts first came to Ireland, but it was probably about 600 B.C. They were not the first settlers, in fact, Ireland has been inhabited since about 6000 B.C., but they did change the pattern of life throughout the country. They brought in new customs and skills, especially the ability to make tools and weapons from iron, and introduced the distinctive Celtic language.

Ireland never formed part of the Roman Empire. The next wave of invaders, the Vikings, did not start raiding until the eighth century, so Celtic customs and the way of life survived relatively undisturbed even though Christianity was introduced in the fifth century.

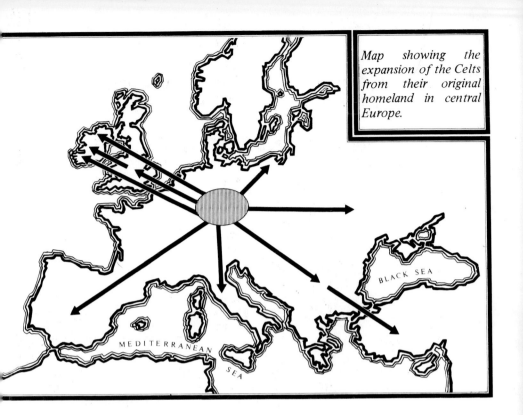

Map showing the expansion of the Celts from their original homeland in central Europe.

BLACK SEA

MEDITERRANEAN

SEA

BONE FLAKE, one of hundreds discovered in a megalithic tomb at Loughcrew, Oldcastle, Their function is unknown and they have not been found on any other site. While the tomb itself dates to 2000 B.C. the ornament on the bone flakes clearly indicate that they belong to Celtic Ireland. The bone in the picture is about 10.16 cm. long and it dates to 1st century B.C.

Reproduced from a woodcut made in Strasbourg in 1513
(from a manuscript in the National Library of Ireland.)

MAPS

Map making began in the Middle East, first with the Egyptians and then the Greeks. Ireland wasn't on the main trading routes, but would still have had contact with European countries. In the second century A.D., a Greek map maker called Claudius Ptolemy plotted the position of Ireland and collected information about the country. This map has been drawn from the information that Ptolemy gave in his writings.

THE COUNTRYSIDE

The Celtic invaders and settlers would have been faced with an Irish countryside much wilder and emptier than it is now. Large parts of the country were covered in forests and there were great areas of marshland and bog. Many places which are now bogland would then have been covered with trees, indeed men cutting turf often find remains of earlier settlements. As well as the forest and bogland there were large open plains where the people grew crops and grazed their animals, and plenty of rivers and lakes to supply fresh water.

Wild animals roamed freely through the countryside and there were numerous varieties of birds and fish. There were great herds of deer, wild boars with long and dangerous tusks, and even wolves in the woods. Flocks of cranes, wild geese and wild swans could be found in the lakes and marshlands, and kites, golden eagles and goshawks were much more numerous than they are now.

The Celts were a farming people and their homes were isolated rather than being grouped together in towns and villages. People could travel fairly easily from one place to another because there were plenty of rough roads and tracks, but if they didn't feel like walking they could go on horseback or in carts pulled by horses or oxen. Rivers were often difficult to cross, there would have been some wooden bridges or ferryboats, but people usually waded across at shallow fords. Causeways made out of layers of trees, brushwood, earth and stones were sometimes built across boggy land. People were expected to try and keep the roads in reasonable condition — an old Irish text stated:

'A road of whatever class must be cleared on at least three occasions, that is, the time of horse racing, winter and war.'

This is an old Irish poem written in the 7th century by a hermit living alone in a woodland. The countryside that he describes would not have changed much since the time of the earliest Celtic invaders.

THE HERMIT'S SONG

A hiding tuft, a green-barked yew tree
Is my roof,
While nearby a great oak keeps me
Tempest-proof.

I can pick my fruit from an apple
Like an inn,
Or can fill my fist where hazels
shut me in.

A clear well beside me offers
Best of drink,
And there grows a bed of cresses
Near its brink.

Pigs and goats, the friendliest neighbours,
Nestle near,
Wild swine come, or broods of badgers,
Grazing deer.

All the gentry of the county
Come to call!
And the foxes come behind them,
Best of all.

To what meals the woods invite me
All about!
There are water, herbs and cresses,
Salmon, trout.

A clutch of eggs, sweet mast and honey
Are my meat,
Heathberries and whortleberries
For a sweet.

All that one could ask for comfort
Round me grows,
There are hips and haws and strawberries,
Nuts and sloes.

And when the summer spreads its mantle
What a sight!
Marjoram and leeks and pignuts,
Juicy, bright.

Dainty redbreasts briskly forage
Every bush
Round and round my hut there flutter
Swallow, thrush.

10

Bees and beetles, music-makers,
Croon and strum;
Geese pass over, duck in autumn,
Dark streams hum.

Angry wren, officious linnet
And black-cap,
All industrious, and the woodpecker's
Sturdy tap.

From the sea the gulls and herons
Flutter in,
While in upland heather rises
The grey hen.

In the year's most brilliant weather
Heifers low
Through green fields, not driven nor beaten,
Tranquil, slow.

In wreathed boughs the wind is whispering,
Skies are blue,
Swans call, river water falling
Is calling too.

(Translated by Frank O'Connor)

11

APPEARANCE

The Celts seem to have been a rather striking people, tall, fair skinned and with fair or reddish hair. They were very concerned with their appearance and took special care of their hair which was usually worn fairly long. They were fond of jewellery and ornaments and the women probably used cosmetics; berry juice to dye their eyebrows and a herb called ruam to redden their cheeks. Personal hygiene was not neglected, there are references to people washing and bathing and using oils and sweet herbs to anoint their bodies after a bath.

There are several descriptions of the Celts by Roman historians; one of them called Strabo remarks that the Celts were figure conscious:

'...they try not to become stout and fat bellied, and any young man who exceeds the standard length of the girdle is fined.'

While another one, Diodorus Siculus gives us a very detailed picture. Diodorus was writing about the Celts who lived in the area now known as France. He called them Gauls, but his remarks apply to all the Celtic peoples.

'The Gauls are tall in stature and their flesh is very moist and white, while their hair is not only naturally blond, but they also use artificial means to increase this natural quality of colour. For they continually wash their hair with lime — wash and draw it back from their forehead to the crown and to the nape of the neck, with the result that their appearance resembles that of Satyrs or Pans, for the hair is so thickened by this treatment that it differs in no way from a horse's mane. Some shave off the beard, while others cultivate a short beard; the nobles shave the cheeks but let the moustache grow freely so that it covers the mouth. And so when they are eating the moustache becomes entangled in the food, and when they are drinking the drink passes, as it were, through a sort of strainer...'

The Celts were said to be great talkers and storytellers. Diodorus Siculus thought that they were boasters as well.

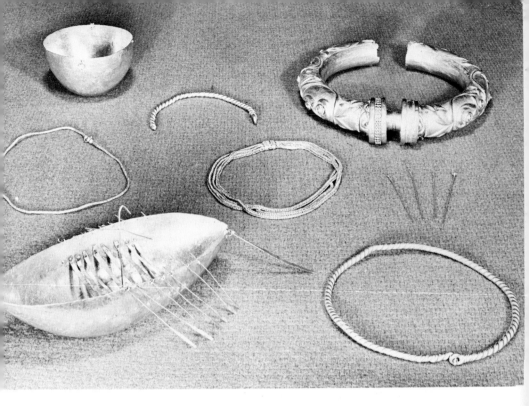

'Physically the Gauls are terrifying in appearance, with deep sounding and very harsh voices. In conversation they use few words and speak in riddles, for the most part hinting at things and leaving a great deal to be understood. They frequently exaggerate with the aim of extolling themselves and diminishing the status of others. They are boasters and threateners and given to bombastic self dramatization, and yet they are quick of mind and with good natural ability for learning.'

Hoard of gold objects found together by two ploughmen at Broighter, near Limavaddy, Co. Derry. Included are (top left) a beaten sheet gold bowl; three fine necklaces and a portion of a fourth; and a superb example of early Irish craftsmanship in the form of a hollow gold collar, the whole surface of which is decorated with raised designs. There is also a small boat complete with steering oar, fourteen rowing oars, seats for oarsmen and mast. The hoard dates to 1st century B.C.

In contrast to the rather fearsome picture painted by Diodorus, this is an eighth century Irish description of a handsome man.

Froech in the dark pool

...He went to come out of the water then. "Do not come out" said Ailill, "till you bring me a branch of that mountain ash on the bank of the river. Beautiful I think its berries". He went away then and broke a spray from the tree, and carried it on his back through the water. And this was what Findabhair used to say afterwards of any beautiful thing which she saw, that she thought it more beautiful to see Froech across the dark pool; the body so white and the hair so lovely, the face so shapely, the eye so blue, and he a tender youth without fault or blemish, with face narrow below and above, and he straight and spotless, and the branch with the red berries between the throat and the white face.

CLOTHING

The Celts wore simple, colourful clothes using the linen and woollen materials that they produced themselves. Men and women both wore tunics and long cloaks fastened with pins or brooches. Sometimes the men wore short, knee length trousers under their tunics as well. Shoes and sandals were made from leather and tied with thongs. Jewellery was very popular and rings, bracelets and torcs were worn by both men and women. A second century writer said:

'They wear ornaments of gold, torques on their necks, and bracelets on their arms and wrists, while people of high rank wear dyed garments besprinkled with gold.'

Archaeologists have found many of these pins, brooches and torcs and some of them can be seen in the National Museum in Dublin.

15

where they lived

RING FORTS

HE CELTS did not live in towns or villages but in isolated farmsteads scattered throughout the country. These farmsteads are generally called forts, though they were not really designed for defence. The forts were mainly circular in design, and the land containing the house would have been surrounded by an earthen bank or stone wall and a ditch. Different Irish terms were used for the forts, those surrounded by an earth bank were commonly called raths, while the terms cathair and caiseal were used for those with stone walls.

Forts varied greatly in size, they were usually 40-50 metres in diameter, though some could be as much as 100 metres across. The surrounding bank of earth or stone would have been quite high, possibly even being topped with a wooden fence. There was only one entrance which was closed at night time. The dwelling house and storage buildings would have been inside the fort, and some of the land outside would have been cultivated. The animals would probably have been brought inside the fort at night to keep them safe from the attacks of wild animals and from thieves.

16

Lismore Fort, Co. Louth. The haystacks give an indication of the scale.

Underground passages or souterains have been found in some of the forts. Their exact purpose is uncertain, but they might have been used as a hide-out in times of danger or just as places for storing food.

The remains of these forts can be seen throughout the country and it has been estimated that there are between thirty and forty thousand — some country people still refer to them as fairy forts and regard them as magic places where humans are not really safe.

The Celtic nobleman or king would have had a much larger fort than the ordinary farmer. Not only would the house itself have been larger but more land would have been enclosed so that there would be space for sports and weapon training, as well as places for the animals. The king would have needed a strong fort that could be defended from his enemies and in which he could provide hospitality for his friends. In a royal fort someone would always have been on watch to guard the entrance and keep a look-out for visitors and troublemakers.

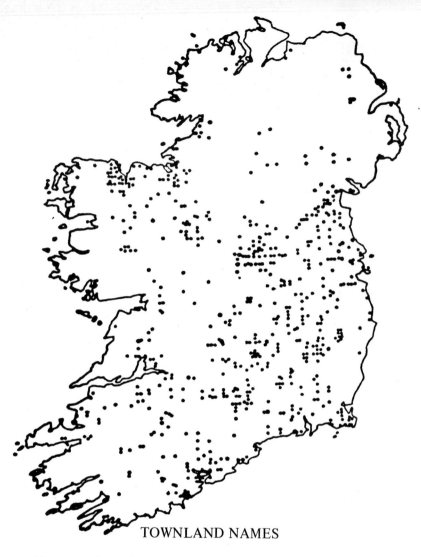

TOWNLAND NAMES

The remains of over thirty thousand Irish ring forts have been found. It would be difficult to reproduce a map showing their distribution. However it is possible to trace the ring forts from townland names since five terms were used to signify forts. These terms are dun, rath, lios, cathair and caiseal. The terms dun, rath, and lios are used for earthen banked forts, cathair and caiseal for stone banked ones. This map shows the distribution of forts by townland name.

polítícal organísatíon

ELTIC IRELAND was divided into about 150 tiny kingdoms called Tuatha and the people within each tuath were divided into four main groups, the king and his family, the nobles, the freemen and the unfree. Each tuath had its own king, who would lead the people into battle and represent them in peacetime, but he did not make the laws or act as judge. The nobles were land-owning families and warriors but druids, poets and some of the craftsmen also belonged to this group. The ordinary freemen were mainly farmers, and beneath them were the unfree people, slaves and bondsmen. A number of tuatha joined or allied together made up a local province which was ruled by a greater king. There would be kings for different provinces but there was no high king, or king of all Ireland. (Some kings afterwards began to claim this title, but not until the eighth century at earliest).

THE FAMILY GROUP

A family group was more important than any one individual in the tuath. In law the family group extended to four generations and included all the descendants of a common great-grandfather, this group was called the derbfine. Land was owned jointly by the group and they

would all have a share in any inheritance.

CHOOSING A KING

Although in theory any member of the royal derbfine could be king, the family chose the person best suited, one who could lead them in battle and manage their affairs in peacetime. There were two main conditions, the king was not to have any deformities or blemishes which might prevent him being a good warrior, or which might make the people laugh at him, and his father and grandfather must have been nobles. Though it was supposed to be a peaceful affair, rivals would often try to maim or kill each other to try and get the kingship for themselves.

THE KING

The king was a very important figure in Irish society, the ruler of his people in peacetime and their military leader in war. He was responsible for any contacts with other kings, either friendly or hostile, but he did not make the laws or usually act as judge. The people believed that the rule of a good king would make the tuath prosperous — the crops would grow well, the seas and rivers would be full of fish, men and animals would be fertile and there would be plenty of food. If the king was unjust there would be war and famine.

The king was often referred to in the laws, and in one instance even his activities were planned.

'There are seven occupations for a king; Sunday for drinking ale, for he is not a lawful chief who does not distribute ale every Sunday; Monday for judgement, for the adjustment of the people; Tuesday at chess; Wednesday seeing greyhounds coursing; Thursday at marriage duties; Friday at horse racing; Saturday at giving judgements.'

The following story from an old Irish manuscript, seems to suggest that only a foolish man would refuse to obey the king.

24

'Eating a mouse includes his tail.'
(Irish; author unknown, 9th – 10th Century).

...'That is true,' said the king, 'this is Lughaidh, and it is through fear of me that they do not name themselves'...

'Well now,' said the king, 'kill me a batch of mice.' Then he put a mouse in the food served to each man, raw and bloody, with the hair on, and this was set before them; and they were told they would be killed unless they ate the mice. They grew very pale at that. Never had a more distressing vexation been put upon them. 'How are they?' said the king. 'They are miserable, with their plates before them.' ... 'Tell them they shall be killed unless they eat.' 'Bad luck to him who decreed it,' said Lughaidh, putting the mouse in his mouth, while the king watched him. At that all the men put them in. There was one poor wretch of them who gagged as he put the tail of the mouse in his mouth. 'A sword across your throat.' said Lughaidh, 'eating a mouse includes its tail'. Then he swallowed the mouse's tail. 'They do as you tell them,' said the king from the door.

'I do as they tell me, too,' said Lughaidh.

'Are you Lughaidh?' said the king. 'That is my name' said Lughaidh...'

THE KING OF CONNACHT
(Translated by Frank O'Connor)

'Have you seen Hugh,
The Connacht King in the field?'
'All that we saw
was his shadow under his shield.'

HOSTAGE CHAIN beautifully made of graduated links with a decorated, hinged, iron collar. As Irish literature indicates, hostages were commonly given as a surety of good behaviour by one king or chieftain to another. This chain was found in the royal crannog of Lagore near Dunshaughlin, Co. Meath and dates to 7th century A.D.

SLAVES

Slaves were kept in some Celtic households, but they don't seem to have formed a large section of the population. They were mainly captives taken in battle and were probably kept as servants in noble households. They would have been given the heavy difficult work to do, ploughing, sowing and harrowing for the men and domestic duties for the women, especially corn grinding with the quern. Slave chains have been found in excavations and there seems to have been some trade in slaves. The Irish term for a female slave was cumal and her value was regarded as equivalent to three cows.

26

BRONZE TRUMPET, an example of excellent craftsmanship of the Celtic metal workers of Ireland. The two portions are each made of sheet metal folded over and secured along their edges by a strip of metal held on the inside by tiny rivets. It dates to 2nd century B.C. and was found in a dried up lake called Loughnashade just outside the bank of the Navan Rath near Armagh. About 2 metres long.

THE LAWS

The old Irish laws are called the Brehon Laws. They were not public laws passed in a parliament and enforced in the courts. They were the records of the old customs of the society, which were handed down orally by the poets and were only finally written down about the seventh century. We cannot know how effective these laws were in practice.

Fasting seems to have been one of the main ways of obtaining justice. A man who had a grievance in law against another would go and fast outside the defendant's house. If the defendant ignored him and refused to pay up he lost his honour. Fasting could also be used to bring some evil on a person, or as a sort of compulsion like a geis, to obtain a request from another.

The laws stated that compensation had to be made for any injury done. This compensation was related to the seriousness of the incident and also to the social rank of the person involved, it was called honour price. A chieftain had a higher honour price than a slave.

27

home life

HOUSES

WELLING HOUSES WERE built inside the fort and were usually circular in design. The walls of these houses were made of stone or wood, the roof supported on wooden poles and probably thatched with straw, reeds or rushes. The floor would have been of earth covered with straw or rushes, though if it became very messy extra clay might be brought into the house and a new surface put down on top of the old one. The fire would usually have been built in the centre of the room with a hole left in the roof through which the smoke would escape.

There were no separate rooms, and bedding would just have been spread around the walls at night, though in richer homes there might have been some partitions or screens to give some privacy. People slept on piles of straw and rushes covered with rugs and skins, the hairier the better. There would have been little furniture apart from a few wooden trestles and stools and cooking utensils.

WASHING AND BATHING

All the evidence that we have from the stories indicates that the Celts were particular about their appearance and washed frequently. It was expected that a host would offer visitors a bath, in fact it was probably very necessary if they had walked along muddy roads to reach him. Large

wooden bath tubs were used and the water would have been heated by throwing in hot stones. If several people were waiting for a bath they would probably have to use the same water. Ash made by burning bracken and briars was made into cakes and used as a soap.

FOSTERAGE

Fosterage was an important aspect of Irish life. Instead of keeping a child at home a man would often send a son or daughter to be brought up with another family. In this way the child would acquire a foster father and mother, and probably foster brothers and sisters. The children might be sent to fosterage at one year of age, and stay until they were considered old enough to marry, seventeen for a boy and fourteen for a girl. Sometimes children would be fostered without payment, but often some type of fee was involved. This fee was paid in land or more usually in cattle and varied according to rank. For the son of the lowest order of chief the fee was three cows, while for a king's son it might be as many as thirty. Higher fees had to be paid for the fosterage of girls because they were regarded as being more troublesome. A man was expected to care for his foster children as if they were his own family and to educate them for their place in life, in return the children were expected to help and support their fosterparents in difficult times.

The children of noble families would be carefully taught, the boys educated in riding, swimming and the use of weapons, the girls in sewing and embroidery. Children of lesser rank would be taught to work on the land and in the house, herding and farmwork for boys, the quern and kneading for girls.

These extracts from the old Irish laws show some of the regulations about fosterage:

'How many kinds of fosterage are there? Two: fosterage for affection and fosterage for payment. The price of fosterage of the son of a chief is three sets; four sets is the price of fosterage of his daughter' (A 'set' was half the value of a milch cow). 'There are three periods at which fosterage ends: Death, Crime and Marriage'.

ROLE OF WOMEN

Women had a very important role in Celtic society, and played an active part in everyday affairs. They had legal rights, and rights to own and inherit property. Women accompanied their husbands into battle and in some cases even joined in the fighting. Some were as skilled in the handling of weapons as men, and indeed Cuchulainn was trained as a warrior by two women — Skatha and Aife. There are descriptions of some of these fierce women in the literature. This one is by Ammianus Marcellinus, another Roman historian.

'Almost all the Gauls are of tall stature, fair and ruddy, terrible for the fierceness of their eyes, fond of quarrelling, and of overbearing insolence. In fact a whole band of foreigners will be unable to cope with one of them in a fight, if he calls in his wife, stronger than he by far and with flashing eyes; least of all when she swells her neck and gnashes her teeth, and poising her huge white arms, begins to rain blows mingled with kicks like shots discharged by the twisted cords of a catapult'.

The Celts had liberal views about marriage. Though it was the general custom to have only one wife, there were exceptions, and a man could have a chief wife and a second wife. If a couple did not suit each other, they could get a divorce without difficulty, by mutual consent, and there is some evidence that couples sometimes got married just for a year.

Extract from the laws:

'What are the marriageable ages?
At the end of fourteen years for the daughter and
at the end of seventeen years for the son'.

SAFETY PIN BROOCH seen from the back; it is made of cast bronze and was found at Navan Rath, Armagh. Date: 1st century B.C.

THE OLD WOMAN OF BEARE

The sea crawls from the shore
Leaving there
The despicable weed,
A corpse's hair.
In me,
The desolate withdrawing sea.

The Old Woman of Beare am I
Who once was beautiful.
Now all I know is how to die
I'll do it well.

Look at my skin
Stretched tight on the bone.
Where kings have pressed their lips,
The pain, the pain.

I don't hate the men
Who swore the truth was in their lies.
One thing alone I hate —
Women's eyes.

The young sun
Gives its youth to everyone,
Touching everything with gold.
In me, the cold.

The cold, Yet still a seed
Burns there.
Women love only money now.
But when
I loved, I loved
Young men.

Young men whose horses galloped
On many an open plain
Beating lightning from the ground
I loved such men.

And still the sea
Rears and plunges into me,
Shoving, rolling through my head
Images of the drifting dead.

A soldier cries
Pitifully about his plight;
A king fades
Into the shivering night.

Does not every season prove
That the acorn hits the ground?
Have I not known enough of love
To know it's lost as soon as found?

I drank my fill of wine with kings,
their eyes fixed on my hair.
Now among the stinking hags
I chew the cud of prayer.

Time was the sea
Brought kings as slaves to me.
Now I near the face of God
And the crab crawls through my blood.

I loved the wine
That thrilled me to my fingertips;
Now the mean wind
Stitches salt into my lips.

The coward sea
Slouches away from me.
Fear brings back the tide
That made me stretch at the side
Of him who'd take me briefly for his bride.

The sea grows smaller, smaller now.
Farther, farther it goes
Leaving me here where the foam dries
On the deserted land,
Dry as my shrunken thighs,
As the tongue that presses my lips,
As the veins that break through my hands.

(Translated by Brendan Kennelly)

Edain the Fairy
(Irish; author unknown; 9th century original)

'. . . He saw a woman at the edge of the spring, with a bright silver comb ornamented with gold, washing her hair in a silver bowl with four golden birds on it, and little flashing jewels of purple carbuncle on the rims of the bowl. She had a shaggy purple cloak made of fine fleece, and silver brooches of filigree work decorated with handsome gold, in the cloak; a long-hooded tunic on her, stiff and smooth, of green silk with embroidery of red gold. Wonderful ornaments of gold and silver with twining animal designs, in the tunic on her breast and her shoulder-blades on both sides. The sun was shining on her, so that the men could plainly see the glistening of the gold in the sunlight amid

33

the green silk. There were two golden-yellow tresses on her head; each one was braided of four plaits with a bead at the end of each plait. The colour of her hair seemed to them like the flower of the water-flag in summer, or like red gold that has been polished.

She was loosening her hair to wash it, and her arms were out through the opening at the neck of her dress. Her upper arms were as white as the snow of a single night, and they were soft and straight; and her clear and lovely cheeks were as red as the foxglove of the moor. Her eyebrows were as black as a beetle's wing; her teeth were like a shower of pearls in her head; her eyes were as blue as the bugloss; her lips were as red as vermilion; her shoulders were high and smooth and soft and white; her fingers were pure white and long; her arms were long; her slender long yielding smooth side, soft as wool, was as white as the foam of the wave. Her thighs were warm and glossy, sleek and white. Round and small, firm and white, were her knees. Her shins were short, white and straight. Her heels were even and straight and lovely from behind. If a ruler were laid against her feet, it would be hard to find any fault with them, unless it should make the flesh or skin swell out on them. The bright blush of the moon was in her noble face; the lifting of pride in her smooth brows; the ray of love-making in both her royal eyes; a dimple of sport in both her cheeks, in which there came and went flushes of fast purple as red as the blood of a calf, and others of the bright whiteness of snow. A gentle womanly dignity in her voice; a steady stately walk, a queenly pace. She was the fairest and loveliest and most perfect of the women of the world that the eyes of men had ever seen; they thought she must be of the fairies...'

JEALOUSY

Love like heat and cold
Pierces and then is gone,
Jealousy when it strikes
Sticks in the marrowbone

(Translated by Frank O'Connor)

A LOVE SONG

Such a heart!
Should he leave, how I'd miss him,
Jewel, acorn, youth.
Kiss him!

(Translated by Brendan Kennelly)

34

HOSPITALITY

The Celts seem to have been very friendly and generous, not likely to turn a visitor away from the door. Strangers would be given food and drink before they were asked their business. Any man who failed to do this would be dishonoured and disgraced. Any special occasion like the return of a hero or a victory in battle was celebrated with a great party or feast. Even ordinary evenings would often be spent eating and drinking while listening to singers and storytellers.

FEASTING

A feast was an occasion for great celebration and rejoicing, though it could often end in bloodshed as well if a hero thought that he wasn't being treated with enough honour and attention. Men and women usually sat round in a circle at a feast, taking their places according to rank and giving the most important or influential man the senior position. The champion warrior was given the best portion of meat, and fights often took place to decide who should receive this. Particular joints of meat were reserved for certain individuals at a feast, e.g. a leg of pork for a king, a haunch for a queen, a boar's head for a charioteer.

Posidonius, a writer who was working between 135 B.C. and 51 B.C. gave this description of Celtic feasts:

'The Celts sit on dried grass and have their meals served on wooden tables raised slightly above the earth. Their food consists of a small number of loaves of bread together with a large amount of meat, either boiled or roasted on charcoal or on spits. They partake of this in a cleanly but leonine fashion, raising up whole limbs in both hands and cutting off the meat, while any part which is hard to tear off they cut through with a small dagger which hangs attached to their sword sheath in its own scabbard... When a large number dine together they sit around in a circle with the most influential man in the centre, ... Beside him sits the host and next on either side the others in order of distinction.... The drink of the wealthy classes is wine imported from Italy or from the territory of Marseilles... The lower classes drink wheaten beer prepared with honey, but most people drink

35

it plain... They use a common cup, drinking a little at a time, not more than a mouthful, but they do it rather frequently'.

OISIN

The teeth you see up here,
    Up in the ancient skull,
Once cracked yellow nuts
    And tore the haunch of a bull.

Savage and sharp and huge,
    Crunching the naked bone,
Every tittle and joint
    Was mince when they were done.

The eyes you see up here,
    Up in the aged skull,
Dull they may seem tonight
    But once they were never dull.

Never in darkest night
    Did they take trip or fall;
Now though you stand so close,
    I cannot see you at all.

The legs you see below,
    Nothing could weary them then;
Now they totter and ache,
    A bundle of bones and skin.

Though now they run no more,
    All their glory gone,
Once they were quick to follow
    The shadow of golden Fionn.

(Translated by Frank O'Connor)

STONE CUP, carved out of a single piece of soap stone, it measures 20.32 cm. across and was found at Ballinenagh, Co. Tipperary.

*ARGE CAULDRON made of thin bronze plates riveted together. This is the sort of
essel frequently referred to in early Irish literature and it could have been used for
oiling meat. From Lack East, Co. Clare, it dates to about the 5th century B.C.
readth about 52 cms.*

FOOD

Milk, cheese and meat formed the main part of the Celtic diet. Bread does not seem to have been eaten in large quantities, but corn was used to make a variety of porridges. Cattle were kept for their milk rather than their meat, and though beef was eaten the animals slaughtered for this purpose would be old or maimed ones or unwanted bull calves. Pork was very popular and seems to have been the main meat eaten at feasts, but mutton and venison were eaten as well.

Milk was an important foodstuff and was consumed in large quantities; it might be drunk fresh, allowed to go sour and eaten as curds, or used to make a variety of cheeses and butter. Porridge was made in many different ways, using grain from oats, barley or wheat. It was mixed with fresh or sour milk, flavoured with honey, salt or herbs, made very thick or almost liquid and could be eaten hot or cold.

Fish were caught in the rivers and lakes and cooked over the fire. The salmon was the most prized of all fish, but trout, sea fish and shell fish were all eaten as well.

There is little evidence in the literature about the vegetables that were eaten, and people probably relied on those that they could gather in the wild rather than growing them themselves. They probably used onions, wild leeks, sorrel, nettles, and watercress. A variety of fruits could have been gathered in the summer, sloe, wild cherry, raspberry, blackberry, strawberry, rowan, crabapple and elderberries, but apples seem to have been the only fruit that was cultivated in any way.

Though the winter months were probably hard, the Celts generally seem to have eaten well. Certainly they do not seem to have wasted food; an old Irish text says:

'Anyone who gives another anything in which there has been a dead mouse or dead weasel, three fasts are laid on him who gives it.. If it is in any other dry food, in porridge or in thickened milk, the part round it is thrown away, the rest is consumed'.

*The seating plan of the banqueting hall at Tara,
from an ancient manuscript.*

orsemen, or charioteers, and ewards :—*cuinn* for them.	Distributors (or dividers) :— a *mael* for them.		Cupbearers:— a *mael* for them Herdsmen :— a *mael* for them.	Charioteers :—crooked bones for them. Steward :—*cuind* for him.
arpers and timpanists:—a g's shoulder for them.	Pipers :— a *colptha* for them.	Fire.	Chess-players :— a *colptha* for them.	Hunters :—a pig's shoulder for them.
ehons :—a *lon-chroichti* for em.	Scolaige :—a *less-croichte* for them.	Fire.	Drink-bearers :—a *les-chroichti* for them.	*Aire forgill* :—a *lon-chroichte* for them.
ofessor of Literature :—a *lon-roichti*. Tanist professor:—a *s-crochait* or *prim-chrochait*.	Artisans :—an *ir-croichte* for them.		Braziers :—an *ir-croichti* for them. Fools :—an *ir-croichti* for them.	*Ruiri* :—a *lon-croichte* for them. Queen and royal *ruireach* :—a *les-croichte* [for them].
lam poet :—a *loarcc* for him. nrudh[poet]:—a crooked bone.	Smiths :—a *mael* for them.	Fire. Vat.	Physicians and mariners : — a *mael* for them.	*Aire ard* :—a *loarc* for them. *Clí* [poets] :—a crooked bone for them.
riugu and aire tuisi :—a *laracc* r them.	Shield-makers :—a *milgit-ain* for them.		Mariners:—a *milgitain* for them.	*Aire tuisi* :—a crooked bone. Historian :—a *loarc* for him.
ugtarsair :—a pig's shoulder. is tanist :—a crooked bone.	Chariot-makers :—a *mil-gitain* for them.	Candle.	*Creacoire* :—crooked bones for them, or pig's *colptha*.	*Aire desa* :—a *colptha* for them. *Dos* [poet] :—a pig's shoulder. Or thus: Carpenters and *airig echta*.
ugurs, druids, and *comail* :— *colptha* for them.	Jugglers :—a pig's *colptha* for them.		Buffoons :—a pig's *colptha* for them.	*Fochloc* [poet] :—an *ir-croichte* for him. Or : *aire desa*.
ouse-builder, carpenter, and uir-churan, and rath-builder:— a *ir-crochti* for them.	Satirists :—the fat [part of the] shoulder for them.	Lamp.	*Braigitoire* :—the fat [part of the] shoulder for them.	Cooks, and *creccoire* or *cornaire* :—*midh mir*.
rumpeters, and footmen, or ouse-builders :—cheering ead for them.				Rath-builder and *oblaire* :— a *milgitain* for them.
ngravers and ring-makers :— *nilgatan* for them.		Common Hall.		*Aire echta* :—a pig's shoulder. *Canu* [poet] :—a crooked bone.
hoe-makers and turners :—the at [part of the] shoulder for hem.	The King's doorkeepers :—and chines for them.		The King's fools :—backs for them.	*Muirighi*, and *clasaighi* :—the fat [part of the] shoulder.

Door.

COOKING

The main way of cooking food was over the open fire; archaeologists have not found remains of ovens in the house sites. Meat was roasted on a spit over the fire, or made into a stew in a cauldron. Bread could be put to bake on a hot flagstone in front of the hearth. However the iron or bronze cooking cauldrons would have been valuable possessions, not easily available, so other methods of preparing food were devised. Remains of ancient cooking places show that hot stones were used to heat water, and roast meat. A wooden trough would be filled with water which was brought to the boil by adding stones which had been heated in the fire, meat could then be put in to cook.

A cooking trough like this was discovered in a bog at Ballyvourney in Co. Cork. It held 500 litres of water and the archaeologists found that this amount could be brought to the boil in thirty minutes by adding stones. Once the water was boiling they only had to add another stone at intervals to keep up the temperature. They cooked a leg of mutton perfectly by wrapping it in straw and then boiling it for 3½ hours in this trough. Meat could be roasted by placing the joint on a hot stone and covering it with a mound of hot stones.

Once prepared the food would have been served simply, possibly in a common bowl or dish. Drinking vessels and bowls were usually made from wood which was easily obtainable rather than metal. Wicker baskets could have been used to contain food as well.

The laws suggested the type of food that children should be given when they were being fostered:

'Stirabout is given to them all; but the flavouring which goes into it is different. Salt butter for the sons of inferior grades, fresh butter for the sons of chieftains and honey for the sons of kings. The food of them all is alike, until the end of the year or three years i.e. salt butter, and afterwards fresh butter to the sons of chieftains and honey to the sons of kings'.

'Stirabout made of oatmeal or buttermilk or water is given

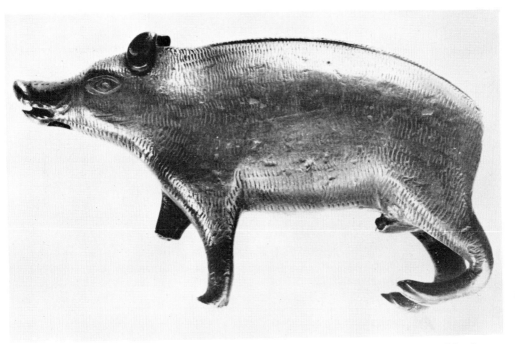

BRONZE BOAR – *a wonderful example of the metal workers art, this piece dates from about 200 B.C. It measures about 7.62 cm. in length.*

to the sons of the Feini grades, and a bare self sufficiency of it merely, and salt butter for flavouring. Stirabout made on new milk is given to the sons of the chieftain grades and fresh butter for flavouring, and a full sufficiency of it is given to them and barley meal upon it. Stirabout made on new milk is given to the sons of kings, and wheaten meal upon it and honey for flavouring'.

The story of Mac Datho's Pig

Mac Datho was a lord of Leinster and his fort was one of the five chief hostels in Ireland. The others were — the hostel of Da Derga at Donnybrook, near Dublin; Forgall Monach beside Lusk; Da Res in Breffni and Da Choga in West Meath. Each hostel had seven doors: seven roads led to it: there were seven hearths and seven cauldrons on each hearth.

An ox and a salted pig went into each cauldron. The traveller who came to the hostel was told to thrust the flesh fork into the cauldron. Whatever came up at the first thrust, that was the share. If nothing came up at the first thrust the wayfarer went hungry.

Mac Datho was a very hospitable man so he was well fitted to be in charge of a hostel. He had a famous hound, called Ailbe, which could run all round Leinster in a day and a boar which was the largest in the world.

One day a messenger came from Queen Maeve of Connaught, asking Mac Datho to sell the hound. Maeve offered six hundred milch cows, a chariot with two of the best horses in Connaught and, at the end of the year as much again.

'That is a good offer!' said Mac Datho politely. But he was fond of the hound and did not want to part with it. As he sat considering, another messenger arrived — this time from King Conor of Ulster. And he brought an offer for the hound.

'Conor of Ulster offers as much as Maeve of Connaught and as well, the friendship and alliance of Ulster'.

'That is also a good offer!' said Mac Datho.

But still he could not bear to part with his hound. For three days he did not eat while he thought and thought what he should do. At night he could not sleep for grieving over the loss of Ailbe and the fear that whatever he did, worse would happen. And he did not know who to ask for advice.

His wife was sorry for him.

'What ails you?' she asked. 'You won't eat the good food that's put before you and you spend the night tossing and turning instead of sleeping'.

'There's a saying' said Mac Datho crossly, 'never trust a slave with money, nor a woman with a secret'.

'You're not getting much comfort from your wisdom!' retorted his wife. 'I might be able to settle your trouble'.

Mac Datho had never known her to give foolish counsel, so he told her the whole story.

'You see the fix I'm in? Which ever one I refuse, will take my cattle and slay my people!'

'That's not so easily settled,' agreed Mac Datho's wife. 'Whatever you do, you can't keep the hound — that's for sure! So give it to both of them and say they must come and fetch it. If there is any fighting to be done, let them fight each other. It's the best advice I can give you and bad's the best!'

Mac Datho thought it good advice and obeyed his wife. He sent for Queen Maeve's messenger and said to him —

'It's taken me a long time to make up my mind. Now I've decided to give the hound to Connaught. But Maeve and her husband, Ailill, must come themselves with their warriors and servants to bring it away and I'll have a feast prepared, worthy of them'.

The messenger rode off delighted, thinking how pleased Maeve and Ailill would be when they heard the news.

The moment he was out of the gate, Mac Datho sent for the Ulster messenger. 'It hasn't been easy for me to agree to give up my hound,' he told him. 'But at long last I see there's nothing else for it. Tell Conor he will be welcome here to the best feast the country has known and let him bring with him his friends and fighting men'.

Away went the Ulster man to King Conor and Mac Datho ordered the feast.

The great boar was killed and roasted: cakes made with

43

44

nuts and honey, stewed meat and soup thickened with herbs, drink of all kinds was laid upon the tables and as the boar was carried into the hall on a shield, the guests marched in.

Conor was surprised to see Maeve and Ailill: they were even more surprised to see him. The Ulstermen and the Connaughtmen sat at different tables. But Conor, Maeve and Ailill sat with Mac Datho at the high table.

Before the feast could begin, the boar had to be carved.

'That is a fine boar!' agreed Ailill. 'How shall it be divided Mac Datho?'

Before the host could answer, Briccriu, whose great pleasure was in making quarrels, leaned forward.

'Isn't it the custom that the bravest man in the company should carve the boar?' he asked. 'All the best warriors of Ireland are here. It should be easy to decide who is the finest fighter!'

'That is a sensible arrangement!' declared Ailill.

'There are many of our Ulster lads here who have fought all through the country,' said Conor.'It should not be hard to choose the best man'.

Along the tables the warriors shouted the brave deeds they had done. Ulstermen glared at Connaughtmen. The spears and swords still leaned against the walls below the shields, but Mac Datho knew it would not be long before they were taken up and used.

At last Ket, one of the Connaughtmen, leaped from his seat and, standing over the boar, knife in hand, challenged each of the Ulstermen to match his brave deeds. One after another, they told their best fights and with every one of them Ket had a braver story to tell. He looked about him triumphantly and was about to carve the boar, when a roar of welcome came from the Ulstermen seated at the end door and in strode Conall of the Victories. He strode up to the boar and Conor, who had been frowning, smiled again.

'I see the feast is ready,' said Conall. 'Who is carving the boar?'

'Ket,' they told him, 'for he is the bravest here!'

'Is that so?' asked Conall.

'It is!' replied Ket. 'And you are welcome to the feast, victorious Conall!'

Conall stood before him.

'And now step away from the boar that I may carve it!' he said.

'Why should I do that?' demanded Ket.

'Because since I first took weapons in my hand I have never passed one day that I did not kill a Connaughtman, nor one night when I did not make a foray on them'.

Ket bent his head.

'You are then a better man than I am' he said. 'Take my place by the boar. But if Aluain, my brother were here, he would match every deed of your with a better, and it is a sorrow and a shame that he is not!'

'Aluain is here!' shouted Conall, and drawing from a bag the head of Aluain he flung it at Ket.

Every man in the hostel sprang to his feet, seized spear or sword and attacked the nearest man in the hostile force. Out from the hall they swept, cutting and thrusting, until King Ailill sprang into his chariot and, with Maeve beside him, shouted to the Connaughtmen to stop the foolish fight and follow.

The Ulstermen pursued them. Ailbe, the hound, excited by the tumult, raced ahead and coming up with the chariot, caught the pole in its teeth. Ailill drew rein but the charioteer raised his sword and struck at the hound with a mighty blow, cutting off its head.

So neither Connaught nor Ulster won the hound and, though Mac Datho lost it, he saved his lands and his people.

from 'Tales of Enchantment' by Patricia Lynch
(Clonmore and Reynolds)

A Fishing Harpoon

46

CARING FOR THE SICK

It was a well established tradition among the Celts to care for those who were sick. According to law a person who had wounded another had to take the victim into his own house and look after him till he recovered. Though he didn't have to do this till a few days after the incident:

'Not removed before the ninth day is any person transfixed by a spear or any invalid of whom it is not known whether he will live or die. For it is wasted labour if anyone maintain a doomed person'.

Certain people were not entitled to sick maintenance:

'There are three men in the territory who have no right to either nursing or fines: A man who refuses hospitality to every class of person, a man who is false to his honour, a man who steals everybody's property — men who do not observe their just obligations'.

The laws stated how the sick were to be treated, and the food that they were to receive:

'Let there be proclaimed what things are forbidden in regard to him who is on his sick bed of pain. There are not admitted to him into the house fools or lunatics, or senseless people or half wits or enemies. No games are played in the house. No tidings are announced. No children are chastised. Neither women nor men exchange blows. No hides are beaten. There is no fighting. He is not suddenly awakened. No conversation is held across him or across his pillow. No dogs are set fighting in his presence or in his neighbourhood outside. No shout is raised. No pigs grunt. No brawls are made. No cry of victory is raised nor shout in playing games. No shout or scream is raised'.

'There are three condiments which the rule of nursing in Irish law excludes: Every salt fare which is prepared with sea produce, the flesh of a whale and of a horse, and honey. For the produce of the sea impels one to drink. Does not horse flesh stir up sickness in the stomach of wounded heroes? Stomachs endure not a storm save people who can retain it. It is not right to give horse flesh to any invalid. Honey disturbs the stomach in which there is looseness of the bowels'.

47

WORK

FORTS AND CRANNOGS were scattered widely throughout the country and as there were no towns or trading centres the people had to be largely self sufficient. Everything that they needed, food, shelter, clothing, tools, weapons etc. they would have to provide themselves. Celtic society was not very free, and much of the heavy menial work would have been done by slaves or those of lesser rank, nevertheless it seems unlikely that the chiefs spent as much time fighting and feasting as the stories might suggest.

CATTLE

The Celts owned great herds of cattle and these were their most valued possessions. Though the animals were kept mainly for their milk rather than their meat, they were one of the chief sources of food, and the whole way of life depended on them. A man's wealth and social standing was measured by the number of cattle that he owned, and prices, wages and marriage portions were all estimated in cows. Cattle raiding was common and was the start of many battles.

It seems likely that many of the animals were killed in the autumn and their meat salted and kept for later use, because grass was in short supply during the winter months. Nevertheless herding the cattle and protecting them from animals and thieves would have been a full time occupation. When a

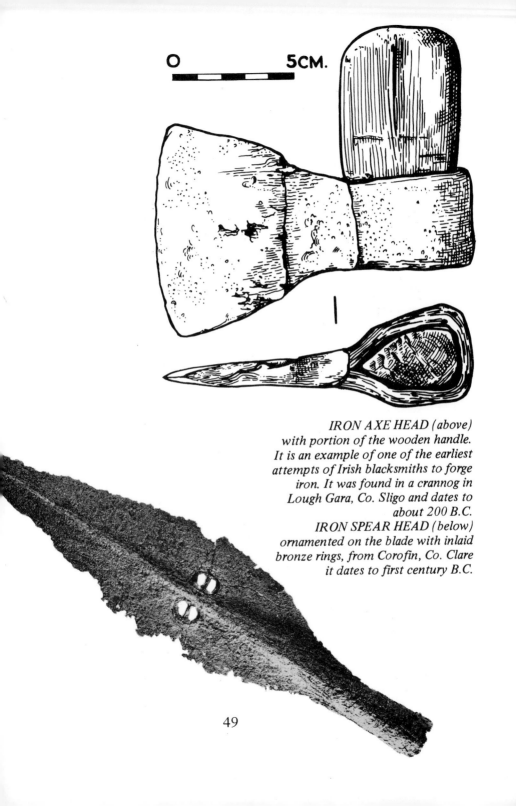

O   5CM.

*IRON AXE HEAD (above)
with portion of the wooden handle.
It is an example of one of the earliest
attempts of Irish blacksmiths to forge
iron. It was found in a crannog in
Lough Gara, Co. Sligo and dates to
about 200 B.C.
IRON SPEAR HEAD (below)
ornamented on the blade with inlaid
bronze rings, from Corofin, Co. Clare
it dates to first century B.C.*

cow was killed it not only provided beef for the household, but a hide which was used for everything from footwear to covering curraghs.

PIGS

Every farmer would have owned some pigs and large numbers of them roamed freely through the woodland, feeding on acorns and anything else that they could pick up. They were easy to manage because they could remain outdoors without shelter for most of the year. Pork seems to have been a most popular meat and it was always supplied at feasts.

These Celtic pigs seem to have been a very vicious breed. The reference to pigs in the stories and writings indicate that they were long snouted, thin, muscular and active, always ready to attack and able to scour the country like hounds.

A contemporary writer Diodorus Siculus said:

'Their pigs are allowed to run wild and are noted for their height, and pugnacity and swiftness. It is dangerous for a stranger to approach them, and also for a wolf'.

HUNTING AND TRAPPING

Hunting was a major sport and leisure time occupation, as well as being a necessity of life. It was the main means of providing extra meat for the home. Deer and wild boar were hunted when food was wanted, but if the men were just out for a day's sport they would chase foxes and hares, or even wolves and badgers. Huntsmen seem to have moved on foot more often than on horseback, but they would always have been accompanied by packs of dogs, usually wolfhounds if large dangerous animals were being chased.

Deer were often caught in elaborate traps as well as being hunted down. One common method was to dig a deep pit, place a trap at the bottom and then cover the entrance with brambles; the deer would step on it unawares and plunge down into the trap.

Birds were caught in a variety of ways, stolen out of nests or brought down in flight by a stone thrown from a sling. In

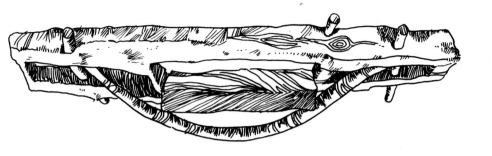

DEER TRAP made from wood. Drawing from the original in the National Museum of Ireland.

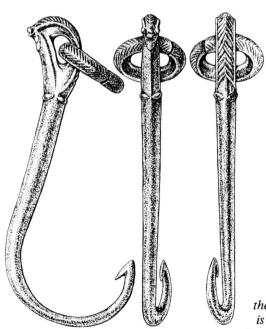

*BRONZE FISH HOOK
— Three different views.
The loop is designed in
the style of an animal's head. It
is about 7.62 cm. high and was
found at Carrownanty, Co. Sligo.*

coastal areas men were sometimes lowered down a cliff face in a basket at the end of a rope, so that they could collect eggs and chicks from the nests.

FISHING

Fish provided a valuable addition to the diet and fishing was a common pursuit with those who had access to rivers, lakes or the sea. Salmon and eels were often caught with a trident spear, but hooks and lines and nets were used as well. A fishing net was often owned in common by the fine or family group of relations and any fish caught would be shared among the group.

MY STORY
(Translated by Brendan Kennelly from an early Irish poem)

Here's my story; the stag cries,
Winter snarls as summer dies.

The wind bullies the low sun
In poor light; the seas moan.

Shapeless bracken is turning red,
The wildgoose raises its desperate head.

Birds' wings freeze where fields are hoary.
The world is ice. That's my story.

WOODEN DUGOUT CANOE. These vessels, used mainly on inland waters, were carved out of a full split oak tree trunk. They were propelled with broad bladed wooden paddles held in two hands by a paddler seated on the bottom. They range in date from the Stone Age down to mediaeval times, and were used to transport people, animals and goods. This example is about 3.65 metres long.

QUERN STONE. This is the upper part of a Quern used about the 1st century A.D. for grinding corn. Note the wooden handle (a modern reconstruction) inserted into the stone. This is an example of the 'bee-hive' type of Quern.

BOATS

The countryside was thickly wooded, and roads often little more than rough tracks, so it must often have been easier to travel by water than on land. The two main types of boat that were used were the curragh and the dugout canoe.

Curraghs are still used in the west of Ireland and they have changed little in design. They were made by stretching hides over a wooden frame and stitching them together with leather thongs. Sometimes two or three layers of hide were used to make the boats stronger and safer.

Dugout canoes were made in large numbers and seem to have been widely used on inland lakes and rivers. They would have provided the main means of communication between a crannog and the shore. Archaeologists have found the remains of many of these canoes varying in length from two to twenty metres. They were made from a single tree trunk, usually oak, and were roughly shaped at either end. The inside would either have been burnt out or chipped away with an axe. It seems that the bottom of the canoes was thicker than the sides; the extra weight would make them easier to right if they capsized.

USING THE QUERN

Much of the routine work about the house was done by the women. One of the main jobs was the preparation of food, often a slow task, especially as the corn used for bread and porridge had to be ground by hand. The small hand mills that were used for this purpose were called querns. They were quite simple in design, two stones the bottom one slightly convex in shape, the upper one concave, were fitted on top of each other, corn was poured in between them through a hole in the top stone, then a handle was fitted in position and pushed round so that the top stone moved over the bottom one. In this way the corn was ground into flour which fell out around the sides of the quern. This rotary quern was a Celtic innovation; in the earlier type called saddle querns, a round stone was merely pushed back and forth over a pile of grain placed in the bottom of a hollow stone. Though most of the grain used would have been ground by hand at home, it is probable that there were a few mills in use. The earliest type was a horizontal water mill, and in these a chute of water was directed against the wheel which turned the mill stones.

WEAVING

The woollen cloth used to make cloaks and tunics would have been woven in the home, usually by women. Simple looms were made from branches, and the strands of wool would have been weighted down with heavy stones. The

55

fabrics would have been dyed with a variety of vegetable dyes and stains before they were made into garments as the Celts were fond of brightly coloured clothes. Saffron made a yellow dye for tunics, seaweeds and lichens could produce purple and reddish colours. Some of the clothes would probably have been embroidered by the women.

FIGHTING

The Celts were a proud, brave people, quick to defend their honour and warlike in spirit. Cattle raids or disputes about the ownership of land or possessions often resulted in great wars that could involve whole provinces. Kings were expected to be skilled at leading men in battle, and the Celtic heroes were always great warriors. Violence broke out easily as the young men trained to use weapons from their boyhood, were always eager to demonstrate their courage and fearlessness in conflict. A 2nd century writer said of the Celts:

'The whole race... is madly fond of war, high spirited and quick to battle.....'

SINGLE COMBAT

The practice of fighting in single combat was quite common and disputes were often settled in this way. Each side would choose their bravest warrior, and these two men would then fight each other to the death. Warriors were quick to fight if they thought that they had been insulted in any way.

'The Celts sometimes engage in single combat at dinner. Assembling in arms they engage in a mock battle drill, and mutual thrust and parry but sometimes wounds are inflicted and the irritation caused by this may lead even to the slaying of the opponent unless the bystanders hold them back'.

(Posidonius)

HEADHUNTING

One of the more unpleasant Celtic customs was to cut the heads off enemies that they had slain in battle. These heads were carried home as trophies, and then would often be left as offerings to the gods.

WEAPONS

Swords and spears were the weapons most commonly used by the Celts, though slings, stones and battle axes were also available. Shields were usually used for protection and helmets and jerkins might have been worn as well, though there are several references in the literature to the Celtic warriors going naked into battle.

This comment was made by Diodorus Siculus:

'Some of them so far despise death that they descend to do battle, unclothed except for a girdle'.

The iron swords were fairly long and bent easily, it seems that they often became twisted after the first blow and had to be straightened with the foot. The spears had wooden shafts and metal heads and were widely used for hunting as well as fighting. The spear heads were either leaf shaped or shouldered. The shields were usually made of alder wood and covered in leather. They were round or rectangular and the hand grip in the centre was protected by an extra piece of wood called a boss.

Light two-wheeled chariots were used by warriors riding into battle. There was room for two men; a warrior and a charioteer. They would drive right up to the enemy, hurling spears at them, then the warrior would often jump down to fight in hand to hand combat, relying on the charioteer to come in and rescue him if he got into difficulties. The fear of invasion and attack was always present.

IRON SWORD with bronze hilt mounts. This is a typical sword of the Celtic people who lived in Ireland; it dates to 3rd century B.C. and was found at Cashel, Co. Sligo.

Leisure

HE ROUTINE OF working, hunting, possibly fighting would have occupied most of the day, but there is plenty of evidence to show that the Celts liked to enjoy themselves as well. Many everyday things could give great pleasure — a good day's hunting with the dogs, a house well thatched or a cloak well made, but above all the Celts seem to have loved an evening of eating and drinking, talking and singing. Feasts for special occasions could often last several days. Poetry and story-telling were an important part of Celtic life and evenings would be spent round a fire listening to the tales of kings and warriors, battles and triumphs. There were no written documents so the only way of learning about the past was to listen to the stories and poems and to try and remember them. Knowledge was passed on from one generation to another in this way.

POETS

A man had to study for many years to become a poet (file) because he had to learn all the traditional stories and poems by heart. However once he had done this he became a very respected man in society. The poets would travel around the country staying with different noble families, entertaining them and also bringing news of affairs in the rest of the country. They were protected by the laws and would have been well looked after though sometimes they were feared as much as respected. As well as telling the traditional stories and poems they would make up new ones, and people were often rather afraid that a poem would be made about them which would make them the laughing stock of the country.

A Roman writer Athenaeus made this reference to a poet:

'A Celtic poet who arrived too late met Louernius and composed a song magnifying his greatness and lamenting his own late arrival. Louernius was very pleased and asked for a bag of gold and threw it to the poet who ran beside his chariot. The poet picked it up and sang another song saying that the very tracks made by his chariot on the earth gave gold and largesse to mankind'.

THE BOORISH PATRON

I have heard that he does not give horses
for songs of praise;
he gives what is natural to him – a cow.

(Irish; author unknown; ninth century)

BRONZE OBJECTS, sometimes known as 'spoons' or 'castanets' their exact function is unknown. They are usually found in pairs, in Celtic countries, in graves of women. Date last century B.C.

GAMES

The Celts seem to have practiced a number of outdoor sports; running, jumping and ball games as well as a form of hurley. In addition gaming pieces and dice have been found and there are references to a board game using wooden pieces that were pegged into position. Two board games called brandub and fidchell were being played in Ireland about the 7th century A.D. and possibly much earlier.

MUSIC

The Celts loved music and no gathering or celebration would be complete without it. They realised how music can affect the feelings and emotions, and the stories often refer to the way musicians calmed individuals or lulled them into sleep.

Several different types of musical instrument were in use, though U-shaped lyres, harps and the timpan were probably the most common. (The timpan was a small stringed instrument played with a bow). Pipes and curved bronze trumpets were also in use — the trumpets were probably used on ceremonial occasions, to signal men in battle or to mark the arrival of an important individual for example. Music was often accompanied by singing and this would provide one of the main sources of entertainment.

OGHAM

The earliest writing in Ireland probably began about 300 A.D. It is called ogham after Ogmios, the Celtic god of writing and was not written on paper but carved onto stone and wood. The alphabet is made up of sets of up to five strokes on, diagonally across, or on either side of a central line — the central line being the edge of a stone. The inscriptions using the writing are carved on standing stones; they begin at the bottom and climb towards the top of the stone and, if necessary, continue down on the opposite side. These standing stones seem to have been used as gravestones and to mark the boundaries of land.

An Ogham stone from Coolmagort and now at Dunloe, Co. Kerry. Early Christian period. Key to Ogham writing (left).

Belief

HE CELTS BELIEVED that magic forces filled every aspect of their lives and surroundings. They thought that the gods were very powerful and tried to keep them in good humour by offering sacrifices. They had many gods and godesses, each one responsible for some aspect of their lives, and they also believed that woods and trees, wells and rivers were often sacred places. The chief god was Dagda, the good god and the father of the people, but there were many others. For example, Morrigan a fierce warrior goddess, and Lug the fertility god celebrated in the August festival, Lughnasa.

The Celts didn't build great temples to their gods, but used groves in the forest or the land beside a sacred pool for their religious ceremonies. Sometimes they carved statues to their gods out of stone or wood, but often they would just use a mishapen tree trunk as an image. Sacrifices were an important part of the religious ceremonies. Animals would be killed but there was probably occasional human sacrifice too.

The Celts believed that the soul did not die but lived on, and for this reason they do not seem to have been afraid of death. They did not think of their gods as remote beings living in a far off heaven, but as magic people who lived in a hill or underground and who could contact mortals if they wished. They believed in a wonderful supernatural world called Tir na nÓg — The Land of Youth. This was a marvellous place, peaceful, untroubled and very beautiful. A place where there was no disaster and no death and where everyone was happy. It was the home of gods but sometimes ordinary people could be taken away there; it would be so pleasant they wouldn't notice the days passing.

DRUIDS

The Druids were the priests of the Celtic religion. They were very learned men who were skilled in magic and they had a very important place in Celtic society. The Celts thought of the world as a magic place and relied on the Druids to advise them so that they would not anger the gods. The Druids would cast horoscopes and foretell the future and so help people to make decisions, even the kings listened to them. They would help to organise festivals and sacrifices and as well as this, they gave legal judgements. Because they were such learned men they were often called in to settle disputes between people, and to decide on rewards and punishments.

Many of the druids were famous teachers, and young noblemen would come to learn from them. A man could only become a druid after long years of study — possibly even as long as twenty years. There were no written documents so everything had to be learnt by heart. A druid would have to memorise all the traditional information and stories about the world, the history of the people, and the gods, so that he could then hand on this information to others.

Strabo the historian, writing in the first century, said of the Celts:

'They used to stab a human being whom they devoted to death in the back with a dagger and foretell the future from his convulsions'.

FESTIVALS

The Celtic year was divided into four parts according to the seasons, and the passage from one part to another was marked by a great festival. These festivals were:

Samain — Imbolc — Bealtaine — Lughnasa

63

Samain — celebrated on November 1st

Imbolc — celebrated on February 1st

Bealtaine — celebrated on May 1st

Lughnasa — celebrated on August 1st

They mainly had a religious significance though there was feasting and merrymaking as well. The festival of Samain was the most important as it marked the end of one year and the beginning of the next. The herds and flocks of animals would be gathered together before the winter, some would be spared for breeding purposes but the majority would be killed. The night before Samain, the time we now celebrate as Hallowe'en, was thought to be a magic time and people would make sacrifices to the gods, hoping to gain good fortune for the coming year. They were specially careful not to do anything that might anger the gods and so bring them misfortune.

The festival of Imbolc was held on February 1st. It was dedicated to the goddess Brigit and seemed to have been connected with the tending of sheep.

The festival of Bealtaine on May 1st was also very important. It marked the beginning of the warm season and the time when the cattle could be driven out to open grazing. Great fires would be lit throughout the country, and the druids would drive the cattle between two great fires to protect them against disease. Mayday has remained a time of celebration.

The festival of Lughnasa was celebrated on August 1st. Sacrifices were made to the god Lug to ensure the ripening of the crops and to gain a good harvest.

BURIALS

We are not exactly certain how the Celts buried their dead, since little evidence remains from this early Iron Age period in Ireland. Archaeologists have found a few examples of cases where the bodies had been cremated and the bones and ashes then buried and the area protected by a small circular ditch — these are called rim barrows. Sometimes a few possessions, jewellery or glass beads were placed beside the ashes. However whole skeletons have occasionally been found, proving that bodies were not always cremated. In addition there is evidence from Europe showing that the Celts also practised a form of chariot burial. Graves have been found where the warrior was laid on his back across the platform of his chariot with his weapons, shield and helmet by his side. Food, wine and fine vessels were often placed in the grave as well so that he could have a feast in the next life.

GEIS (plural 'gessa')

The word 'geis' means 'taboo' or 'prohibition'. Certain actions or objects were regarded as 'gessa', and to ignore them would bring misfortune or bad luck of some kind on the individual who did so. Usually 'gessa' were restrictions that applied to a particular person.

Examples

It was 'geis' for anyone to turn the left side of his chariot towards Emain Macha.

It was 'geis' for Cuchulainn to eat dog's flesh.

It was 'geis' for the King of Tara to be still in bed at sunrise in the plain of Tara.

It was 'geis' for Conaire whose father was a bird to hunt birds.

STONE HEAD. A view of a carved stone head found at Corravilla, Co. Cavan. It dates from the 2nd or 1st century B.C. and was most likely the head of a pagan god.

THE CHILDREN OF LIR

In the days when Ireland was inhabited by two races of people, the People of Dana or the De Danaan, and the Milesians, these two races agreed to divide the country between them so that they would no longer fight about territory.

They agreed that the Milesians would take the upper half, the half above the ground, and that the De Danaans would have the territory under the ground.

The De Danaans chose as their king Bov the Red, who was a very wise and noble man. All his subjects were loyal to him except Lir, the father of Manannan Mac Lir, the sea god. Lir was offended because he had not been chosen as king himself and from the day that Bov the Red became king, Lir avoided going to court and ignored him.

Some years later, Bov the Red sent for Lir and asked him if he would like to marry one of his three foster daughters. Bov hoped that this would give Lir a chance to forget his disappointment and become friendly once again. And indeed it did, Lir was so pleased to hear from Bov that he decided to set out immediately for the palace on the shores of Lough Derg.

Lir and his followers were given a great welcome when they arrived and a feast was prepared for them. The three foster daughters were present during the meal, and when everybody had eaten the king invited Lir to take his choice of the three girls. As all three were very beautiful it was not an easy decision, but eventually he decided to choose the eldest one, Eve.

Lir and Eve were married that same day and two weeks later Lir brought his bride home to Shee Finnehy.

After some time Eve gave birth to twins, a boy and a girl whom they called Aed and Finola. Lir loved his wife and children dearly and was very happy. Two years later, Eve gave birth to another pair of twins, two sons whom they named Fiacra and Conn. But sadly, Eve died soon after their birth. Lir was heartbroken at losing her, and he worried too about his children who were left without a mother.

67

Not long afterwards King Bov, who was sad to hear of Eve's death, sent a message to Lir asking him if he would like to marry Eva, the second foster daughter. Lir agreed, hoping that Eva would fill the empty place in the house.

So Lir went again to Bov's palace, married Eva and brought her back home with him. She looked after the children well and they loved her dearly in return. These children gave Lir great happiness, indeed he loved them so much that he liked them to sleep in a room near his own. Every morning when they awoke he played with them and told them stories. King Bov their grandfather was very fond of them too and they visited him frequently. They were beautiful and affectionate children, and everyone who knew them loved them.

Unfortunately, as time went on, Eva began to resent the care that was lavished on the children. She was jealous because Lir loved them so much and felt that even her father paid more attention to his grandchildren than to her, his own daughter. Slowly she began to hate the children till finally she could not bear to see them around the house and began to plan how she could be rid of them altogether. Finally her plans were made. One day she asked for her chariot to be brought round to the door and then called the children and told them that she was taking them to see their grandfather. So Aed, Finola, Fiacra and Conn got into the chariot with their stepmother and they set out on the journey.

They had only travelled a few miles from the palace when Eva stopped the chariot and tried to persuade her servants to kill the children. However, they were horrified at her wicked suggestion and refused to do as she asked, so they all journeyed on until they reached Lake Derravaragh in the middle of Ireland. Eva ordered everyone to get out of the chariot here, and she brought the four children down to the lakeside to bathe while the horses were resting. They went into the lake, and as soon as Eva saw that they were in the water she chanted a spell over them, and hit each of them with a druid's wand. Immediately Aed and Finola, Fiacra and Conn were changed into four beautiful white swans.

When they realised what had happened these four swans

69

looked sadly at their stepmother, and then Finola said 'Why have you done this to us Eva? We loved you, and we thought that you loved us. What did we do to deserve such a dreadful punishment?'

Eva forgot her jealousy as she suddenly realised what a terrible thing she had done, but it was too late to change the spell. The children had been condemned to a long exile, they had to spend three hundred years on Lake Derravaragh, three hundred years on the Sea of Moyle, and three hundred years on Inish Glora on the Western Sea. They would remain as swans until a prince from the north married a princess from the south, and until Christianity came to Ireland. Eva tried to lessen the suffering she had caused them by promising that though outwardly they would have a swan's shape, their personalities would be unchanged. They would still be able to talk and to make music. Then Eva got back into her chariot and continued her journey to her father's house. The four swans were left behind on the lake.

King Bov was surprised to see her arrive alone, especially when she said that Lir had not allowed the children to come with her, but he soon heard the true story. When he realised what had happened to his grandchildren he was heartbroken, and was determined that Eva should suffer for her evil deed. As a punishment he cast a spell over her and changed her into a demon spirit.

Afterwards Bov the Red, Lir and some of the nobles went to the shores of Lake Derravaragh. They made camp and settled there so that they could be near the swans and keep them company. In this way the next three hundred years on Lake Derravaragh passed pleasantly — the swans had friends around them, and were able to spend the days talking and making music — music so beautiful that it charmed everyone who heard it.

Finally however, the time came for them to move on to the Sea of Moyle. The four swans, Aed and Finola, Fiacra and Conn, were sad at this because they had been almost as happy on Lake Derravaragh as they had been as children at home, but they could not avoid the spell that had been placed on them.

Early one morning, having spoken to their father and friends for the last time, the swans sang a beautiful song in farewell, and then flew away from the lake, north towards the Sea of Moyle.

The four were depressed and miserable when they arrived on the Sea of Moyle. It was cold and stormy and the only company they had there were the shrieking sea-gulls and the seals. They missed their friends and they seldom talked or sang. They spent many lonely days and nights in this un-inhabited place, but at last the 300 years passed.

The time came to go to Inish Glora and the swans decided to visit Shee Finnehy, their father's home, on the way. It was so long since they had seen it, that they were really happy and excited as they flew south. But when they came near, and looked down they could not find any sign of Lir's palace. They searched everywhere for some trace but in vain. They walked on the hill where the palace had stood but they only found a few ruined walls, overgrown with nettles. They realised sadly that their old home had gone.

Next morning they continued their journey to Inish Glora and landed on a small lake there. It was a much more pleasant place than the Sea of Moyle, the climate was quite gentle and there were thousands of birds in the area — birds that gathered to listen to the swans when they were singing their sad songs.

By this time Christianity had come to Ireland. St. Patrick was travelling throughout the country preaching to the people and building churches and monasteries. One of his followers, a man called Kemoc, built a church on Inish Glora. One morning, soon after he arrived, the four children of Lir were woken up by the sound of the church bell. They were terrified because they had never heard anything like it before. Finola finally realised what it was and she was happy because it was one of the things that could break the spell that Eva had put on them so many years earlier. When she told the others this they began to sing with joy, and the sweet sound of their music reached Kemoc who was praying in his church on the far side of the lake. He went down to the shore and spoke to the swans, asking them if they really were

71

the children of Lir, famous throughout the country for their singing. They told him that they were indeed these children, and he was able to say that the spell would soon be broken. He would look after them until it was removed.

So the swans came ashore and went to Kemoc's house and lived with him there. He taught them about the teachings of Christ, they would join him in his prayers and the days passed happily.

However, a final thing was necessary before the spell could be broken — a princess from the south would have to marry a prince from the north. At this time Decca, daughter of Finmin, King of Munster, had just married Largen, King of Connaught. When Decca heard of the singing swans living on Inish Glora she was determined to capture them. She asked Largen to get the swans for her and he sent a message to Kemoc asking him to catch them. Kemoc refused. When the King heard this, he became very angry and went to Inish Glora himself to get the swans. He dragged them out of the little church where Kemoc had put them for safety. But he had only brought them a short way from the church door when their feathers dropped off and they became human again. Finola was a frail, white-faced old woman, and her three brothers were feeble old men, grey-haired, bony and wrinkled. When the King saw this he was very frightened and returned to his wife to tell her what had happened. The children of Lir asked Kemoc to baptize them because they felt they would die soon, and indeed they died peacefully a short time later. Kemoc buried them side by side in one grave, and he wrote their names on a tombstone over the grave —

"Aed, Finola, Fiacra and Conn — the Children of Lir"